Introduction

Brewing mead is simple, fun, and delicious! Mead is one of the oldest fermented beverages in human history, and nearly every culture in the world has some variation on the basic concept. With popularity of certain TV shows like Game of Thrones and Vikings, the idea of drinking mead has become something of a trendy thing at the moment. While this is wonderful, since it is revitalizing interest in a wonderful beverage, it has spawned a lot of really bad, commercially produced meads. There is no excuse for drinking bad mead when it is so simple to make at home.

History

The earliest known meads were natural fermentation's that occurred when beehives built in hollowed out trees flooded during spring rains and were exposed to wild yeasts. Nomadic tribes collected the resulting liquor and consumed it as part of their seasonal diet. Later, honey was intentionally fermented around the world from Africa to Europe and all the way to Asia.

Mead making is generally considered to have reached its pinnacle during the so-called Viking Age, roughly from about 800 CE to 1200 CE. While the popularity of mead during this time period can't be denied, it was brewed through the High Medieval era and into Victorian times. Even today, mead making continues internationally on a hobby and commercial scale.

Over the last decade or so, the popularity of mead has grown again, with more commercial meaderies cropping up all over the world and especially in the United States. Sadly, the consensus amongst most mead drinkers is that the majority of commercial meads are at best sub par and at worst utterly undrinkable. While there are some notable exceptions to this, the general preference seems to be for artisan meads lovingly handcrafted by enthusiasts of beverage.

<u>Tools</u>

The tools for brewing mead can be as simple or as complex as the beverage itself. To get started, let's keep it simple. You will need a few things that are easy to either buy locally or order online.

- **2 six-gallon, food safe buckets fitted with airtight lids designed to accept airlocks.** My recommendation is Ale Pale or a similar product. These can be ordered online or, if you are more economically conscious, purchased locally from brewing supply stores.
- **1 six-gallon aluminum or stainless steel pot.** Unused turkey fryers work well too. These are available in nearly every department store, big box store, online, or in local hobby or brewing supply stores.
- **1 small, linen bag to contain herbs and spices.** Bags like this can easily be found wherever you purchase your other brewing supplies or at any higher-end coffee or tea shop.
- **1 large, fine, wire mesh strainer to separate out any fruit solids when racking.** Brewing supply

stores, online suppliers, and cooking stores should have these readily available for purchase.

- **Appropriately sized airlocks for your brew buckets.** These should be listed on the same page as your brew buckets or, if you are shopping at a physical store, they should be nearby where you found your buckets.

- **1 beer and wine hydrometer, which is available on line or from a brewing supply store**. Make certain if you are ordering online that you purchase a *beer and wine hydrometer*, not a distillers hydrometer. It is important to purchase the correct one, as they are calibrated for very different tasks.

- **1 graduated cylinder.** Some hydrometers come with a graduated cylinder. If not you will need one in order to take an accurate reading. If you cannot find one or you are not worried about determining ABV and residual sugar accurately, you can get away with taking a less accurate reading by using a large pitcher

- **1 auto siphon,** which will be available online or at a brewing supply store.

- **3 feet of food grade, plastic tubing in the same diameter as your auto siphon**, which should be listed right next to the auto siphons on any website selling this piece of gear or on the same shelf as your auto siphon in your local supply store.

- **1 bottling wand**, which should also be available on the same package as the auto siphon and plastic tubing or on the same shelf as the other two pieces of gear.

- **A corker or beer bottle caper, depending on the type of bottle you will be using.** I use a Portuguese floor press which I purchased locally, simply because I got sick of using a hand corker. I do not use beer bottles for my mead, but if you do, a hand caper should be all you need.

- **Bottles, either beer bottles or 750ml wine bottles.** I find that, for most batches, 750 ml bottles are ideal, though when I make more expensive or complex batches, I use 375ml bottles, which take the same size cork as the larger 750ml bottles.

- **Brewing supply sanitier**, which is readily available wherever you are purchasing your brewing supplies.

- **1 microwave safe vessel** you can neatly and easily pour warmed water out from into another container.

<u>Types of Mead</u>

Mead, in its simplest form, contains only three ingredients: honey, water and yeast. Many variations on this exist with additional ingredients added to create more complex and in depth flavors. Often times these variations came about because honey was scarce, and additional sugars were needed to provide a suitable fermentation. These ingredients can include beet sugar, fruit, malt, or even some vegetables or gourds. Spices and herbs were also added to create more complex flavors or derive certain benefits from the herbs. These can include cinnamon, cardamom, allspice, vanilla, nutmeg, pink peppercorns, ginger and hops.

For the purposes of this book, we will focus only on the four most basic variations on mead: simple honey mead, fruited mead, spiced mead, and fruited mead with spices. These meads are all relatively simple to make and yield delicious results.

Ingredients

When you select your ingredients, try to purchase high quality, locally-produced fruit and honey. While this means that you will be limited to brewing seasonally, the quality of your base components will affect the overall quality of your end product. Locally-produced honey can be quite expensive, so for your first batch, while you are deciding if this is a hobby that is right for you, buying mass-produced and distributed honey can make more financial sense.

If you decide to go the mass produced honey route, make certain any honey you purchase comes from a region that actually produces honey. Synthetic honey is often imported from China and yields a vastly inferior product with a less desirable taste. Also, in many cases, the actual ingredients in synthetic honey are unknown and may pose a health risk when consumed or fermented.

Clean, filtered water will be best for making your mead. If you have a well that produces good water, then this will work fine. If however, you live in an area where you have city or town water, I recommend purchasing bottled water to brew with, as chlorination and other contaminants will affect fermentation and flavor.

Selecting your yeast is an important, but often confusing, step in the brewing processes. You can purchase mead yeast, cider yeast, white wine yeast, red wine yeast, champagne yeast, beer yeast, ale yeast and a thousand variation of each one. This is to say nothing of baker's yeast, which we will be using for every recipe I present here.

You can begin experimenting with different yeasts once you have a feel for the basic process. Changing your yeast will change the flavor, alcohol content, residual sugars, viscosity, and clarity of your end product. Some yeasts will also require the use of specific nutrients and acids. It can get quite complicated, and since that is the antithesis of what this is about, we will avoid it all and stick to simple bread yeast.

Process

Fermentation

Fermentation takes place when yeasts are exposed to a ready supply of digestible sugars. Alcohol and CO_2 are the byproducts of the yeast eating away at the sugars as they ferment. When the alcohol levels in a fermentation rise to a certain point, it creates an environment where yeasts can no longer survive, and fermentation ceases. Different strains of yeast have differing levels of alcohol tolerance. Beer and cider yeasts have relatively low tolerances, while white and red wine yeasts can have much higher tolerances, and champagne yeasts typically have the highest. Bread yeasts usually have tolerances lower then beer yeasts, though I have seen them produce products with upwards of 10% ABV, putting them in the realm of wine yeasts.

What this means for you is bread yeast won't be able to eat as much sugar before the alcohol levels rises too high for the yeast to continue to survive. This will leave you with a higher amount of residual sugar, resulting in a sweeter wine. You will also be left with stronger residual flavors from any fruits you use in your fermentation.

Yeast thrives at temperatures between 45° and

75° Fahrenheit. It also does much better in environments where the temperature is steady, and fluctuations are kept to minimum. Basements that maintain consistent temperatures are ideal for fermentation as are interior closets and wall spaces on the far opposite side of kitchens from stoves and heaters. Fermentation's that occur at lower temperatures, say between 37° and 45° Fahrenheit, happen much, much slower and yield a distinctive uniqueness of flavor. The process is called lagering and is found most often in beer making. Higher temperatures expedite the fermentation process to a point, however, it can have severe negative consequences on the flavor of your final product.

Honey can be notoriously hard to ferment. Historical records indicate large scale batches of mead were brewed in three months cycles. With modern equipment and chemistry, you can expect your timetable to be much shorter than three months, but mead will likely take longer then beer to ferment completely.

Expect fermentation to begin within twenty-four hours of adding your yeast to a batch. That initial fermentation will last anywhere from two to four weeks. You will know the fermentation has slowed down when you no longer see a constant stream of bubbles passing through your airlock. When your fermentation has slowed significantly, it is time to rack your mead.

Racking Your Mead

Place your primary fermentation vessel on a counter top where you have room to work and where it won't be in the way. You will want to leave it there for twenty-four hours to allow the yeast to settle back to the bottom.

Before beginning the racking process, you must sterilize your secondary fermentation vessel as well as your auto siphon and the length of plastic tubing. Once that is done, carefully remove the lid from your primary fermentation vessel and set it aside where it won't drip or get any sticky residue on a hard to clean surface. Make certain the small, spacer cap has been removed from the bottom of the auto siphon and that the plastic tubing is securely attached to the auto siphon's spout. If you are making a fruited mead, this is the point where you will separate the liquid from the fruit. The fruit pieces will be left behind after racking.

Place the auto siphon in your primary fermenter, place your tube into your clean, secondary fermenter, and use the auto siphon to transfer the mead from your primary vessel to your secondary vessel. You may have to cover the open end of your tubing with your thumb in order to create the vacuum needed for the siphon to work. The goal here is to transfer very little yeast from the primary to the secondary vessel while still transferring enough to allow the secondary fermentation to complete.

Your secondary fermentation should complete within two to four weeks. At that point, you can rack your mead a second time, using the spacer cap for your auto siphon this time, to transfer even less yeast. This can be beneficial, though it isn't necessary.

Regardless of whether or not you decide to rack for a second time, at this point, your yeast should start to fall out of mead. This means that it settles to the bottom and the mead becomes increasingly clearer and less cloudy. You can help this process along by using clarifying agents like bentonite clay. Any clarifying agent will have specific instructions on how to use that product, and they should be followed exactly.

Bottling

To bottle your mead, you will need roughly twenty-four, 750 ml wine bottles or forty-eight 375 ml wine bottles or beer bottles. These will all need to be sanitized, and I recommend running them through the dishwasher *without soap* as well, to allow them to be heated with both hot water and through the drying cycle.

Next, move your fermentation vessel onto a counter where it can sit for twenty-four hours, allowing any floating yeast particles to filter out. Now, make certain your bottling wand is firmly attached to plastic tubing and that the tubing is still securely attached to the auto siphon. Use the auto siphon to form a vacuum, and place the bottling wand into one of your bottles. By gently pressing down on the wand, you will allow the mead to flow into the bottle. Once the bottle is filled within an inch of the top, lift up on the wand, and remove it from the bottle. Repeat the process again with your next bottle.

Removing the wand allows the level of liquid to settle back down in the bottle, leaving an air gap that will help prevent the bottle from exploding or popping the cork if there is still any active yeast in the bottled mead.

Once all of your bottles are filled, use your corker or caper to cork or cap the bottles. They are now ready to be stored for aging. Alternatively, they can be consumed now. Mead is very drinkable when first bottled. If you are going to store it, bottles should be stored on their side so a small amount of the mead is in contact with the cork, preventing it from drying out. Corks that dry out can crumble, letting air in and causing your mead to turn to vinegar. Storing and aging mead should be done where sunlight can't reach the bottles and the temperature remains cool, but doesn't drop to freezing.

<u>Recipes</u>

Basic Mead

Ingredients

- 3lbs of honey per gallon of water, (15lbs for a 5-gallon batch). This will yield a very sweet mead, comparable to a dessert wine. You can adjust the quantity up or down depending how you like the results of the 3lbs per gallon recipe.
- 5 gallons of clean, room temperature water
- 1oz of dry, instant, bread yeast

Instruction

- Follow the instructions on whatever sanitizing product you purchased and sanitize ALL of your brewing equipment. Harmful bacteria and wild yeast strains can ruin an otherwise very successful batch.

!!!IMPORTANT!!! *If you are using aluminum pot to prepare you batch in, DO NOT USE any bleach/chlorine-based sanitizing agent. It will discolor your pot and can cause off flavors in your mead.*

- Warm up your bottles of honey in warm tap water. You will want to make sure your containers are still tightly sealed for this step. You simply want your honey to flow easily out of the container, leaving as little behind as possible.

- Pour the warmed honey into your 6-gallon pot. *DO NOT THROW OUT THE CAP OR LID!* If you are using bottled water, use your microwave safe vessel to heat up some of your bottled water. You don't want to boil the water, simply warm it up. Then pour it into your honey container, place whatever lid or cap it came with back on, and shake the container gently. You are trying to dissolve the last of the honey into the warm water. Then pour this water and honey into your 6-gallon pot.

- Place your 6-gallon pot on the stove and set the burner temperature to medium high. You will need to keep a close watch on your honey and water mixture since when it starts to come to a boil, the sugars can begin to caramelize and bubble up and over the edges of your pot. This creates a huge, sticky mess, can lead to fires if you are using an open flame burner, or burn you badly if it gets on your skin. Even if it doesn't cause a fire or burn you, burning your sugars can lead to strong, burnt flavors in your mead, which are undesirable.

- Once your honey and water mixture begins to boil, turn down the heat until it is just barely bubbling. Skim off any brown or discolored foam that rises to the surface. This is especially important if you are using raw or unprocessed honey, as what you see coming to the top is impurities that are harmless if consumed but inhibit fermentation.
- Simmer your honey between twenty minutes and one hour. Then cover the pot with a lid, and let it cool to room temperature. If this mixture is poured into a plastic brew bucket while still too hot, it can damage the plastic, causing off flavors and a poorly sealing lid.
- Once your mixture has cooled to room temperature, pour it into your primary fermentation vessel.
- Top up your fermentation vessel to the five gallon mark with your remaining water.
- Add in your yeast.
- Fill the small cavity on your airlock with water.
- Place your lid on your bucket.
- Gently fit your airlock into the pre-drilled hole in the bucket lid. It should be fitted with a rubber

gasket to make the seal airtight. Twist the airlock into place with a gentle downward pressure to avoid damaging the seal.

- Once the lid and airlock are firmly in place, and the vessel is completely sealed, give the bucket a gentle shake to aerate the yeast and get it mixed in completely.
- Place your fermentation vessel in area that will maintain a steady temperature between 45° and 75° Fahrenheit.
- Once the initial fermentation has finished, follow the racking instructions as they are outlined above.

Apple Mead

Ingredients:

- 3lbs of honey per gallon of water (15lbs for a 5-gallon batch). This will yield a very sweet mead, comparable to a dessert wine. You can adjust the quantity up or down depending how you like the results of the 3lbs-per-gallon recipe.
- 5 gallons of clean, room temperature water
- 1oz of dry, instant, bread yeast
- 2 ½lbs of Granny Smith Apples
- 2 ½lbs Macintosh Apples

Instruction:

- Follow the instruction on whatever sanitizing product you purchased, and sanitize ALL of your brewing equipment. Harmful bacteria and wild yeast strains can ruin an otherwise very successful mead.

!!!IMPORTANT!!! *If you are using aluminum pot to prepare you batch in, DO NOT USE any bleach/chlorine-based sanitizing agent. It will discolor your pot and can cause off flavors in your mead.*

- Peel, core, and cut your apples into small pieces, roughly ½ inch square.
- Warm up your bottles of honey in warm tap water. You will want to make sure your containers are still tightly sealed for this step. You simply want your honey to flow easily out of the container, leaving as little behind as possible.
- Pour the warmed honey into your 6 gallon pot. *DO NOT THROW OUT THE CAP OR LID!* If you are using bottled water, use your microwave safe vessel to heat up some of your bottled water. You don't want to boil the water, simply warm it up. Then pour it into your honey container, place whatever lid or cap it came with back on and shake the container gently. You are trying to dissolve the last of the honey into the warm water. Then pour this water and honey into your 6-gallon pot.
- Add in your chunked apples
- Place your 6-gallon pot on the stove and set the burner temperature to medium high. You will need to keep a close watch on your honey and water mixture, since when it starts to come to a boil, the sugars can begin to caramelize and bubble up and

over the edges of your pot. This creates a huge, sticky mess, can lead to fires if you are using an open flame burner or burn you badly if it gets on your skin. Even if it doesn't cause a fire or burn you, burning your sugars can lead to strong, burnt flavors in your mead, which are undesirable.

- Once your apple, honey and water mixture begins to boil, turn down the heat until it is just barely bubbling. Skim off any brown or discolored foam that rises to the surface. This is especially important if you are using raw or unprocessed honey, as what you see coming to the top is impurities that are harmless if consumed, but inhibit fermentation.

- Simmer your honey for between forty-five minutes and one hour. It is important to make sure your apples have been gently boiled in order to kill any wild yeast still on the apple. Apples naturally have a high quantity of natural yeast strains on them, and this can lead to vinegar or just foul tasting meads if you are not careful. Then, cover the pot with a lid, and let it cool to room temperature. If this mixture is poured into a plastic brew bucket while still too hot, it can damage the plastic, causing off flavors and a poorly sealing lid.

- Once your mixture has cooled to room temperature, pour it into your primary fermentation vessel.

- Top up your fermentation vessel to the five gallon mark with your remaining water.
- Add in your yeast.
- Fill the small cavity on your airlock with water.
- Place your lid on your bucket.
- Gently fit your airlock into the pre-drilled hole in the bucket lid. It should be fitted with a rubber gasket to make the seal airtight. Twist the airlock into place with a gentle downward pressure to avoid damaging the seal.
- Once the lid and airlock are firmly in place, and the vessel is completely sealed, give the bucket a gentle shake to aerate the yeast and get it mixed in completely.
- Place your fermentation vessel in area that will maintain a steady temperature between 45° and 75° Fahrenheit.
- Once the initial fermentation has finished, follow the racking instructions as they are outlined above.

Spiced Mead

Ingredients;

- 3lbs of honey per gallon of water (15lbs for a 5 gallon batch). This will yield a very sweet mead, comparable to a dessert wine. You can adjust the quantity up or down depending how you like the results of the 3lbs-per-gallon recipe.
- 5 gallons of clean, room temperature water
- 1oz of dry, instant, bread yeast
- 2 vanilla beans
- 6 whole cloves
- 6 allspice berries
- 1 cinnamon stick

Instruction;

- Follow the instruction on whatever sanitizing product purchased, and sanitize ALL of your brewing equipment. Harmful bacteria and wild yeast strains can ruin an otherwise very successful mead.

!!!IMPORTANT!!! *If you are using aluminum pot to prepare you batch in, DO NOT USE any bleach/chlorine-based sanitizing agent. It will discolor your pot and can cause off flavors in your mead.*

- Use a sharp knife to carefully split the vanilla beans down the middle lengthwise, then, use the back of the knife to scrape the interior of the bean. Place the scrapings from the interior of the bean into your 6-gallon pot. Place the scraped beans into the linen bag along with the remainder of the spices. Tie the bag closed and place it into the pot as well.
- Warm up your bottles of honey in warm tap water. You will want to make sure your containers are still tightly sealed for this step. You simply want your honey to flow easily out of the container, leaving as little behind as possible.
- Pour the warmed honey into your 6-gallon pot. *DO NOT THROW OUT THE CAP OR LID!* If you are using bottled water, use your microwave safe vessel to heat up some of your bottled water. You don't want to boil the water, simply warm it up. Then pour it into your honey container, place whatever lid or cap it came with back on, and shake the container gently. You are trying to dissolve the last of the honey into the warm water. Then pour this water and honey into your 6-gallon

pot.

- Place your 6-gallon pot on the stove and set the burner temperature to medium high. You will need to keep a close watch on your honey and water mixture, since when it starts to come to a boil, the sugars can begin to caramelize and bubble up and over the edges of your pot. This creates a huge, sticky mess, can lead to fires if you are using an open flame burner or burn you badly if it gets on your skin. Even if it doesn't cause a fire or burn you, burning your sugars can lead to strong, burnt flavors in your mead, which are undesirable.
- Once your honey and water mixture begins to boil, turn down the heat until it is just barely bubbling. Skim off any brown or discolored foam that rises to the surface. This is especially important if you are using raw or unprocessed honey, as what you see coming to the top is impurities that are harmless if consumed, but inhibit fermentation.
- Simmer your honey between twenty minutes and one hour. Then, cover the pot with a lid and let it cool to room temperature. If this mixture is poured into a plastic brew bucket while still too hot, it can damage the plastic, causing off flavors and a poorly sealing lid.
- Once your mixture has cooled to room temperature, remove the cloth bag and pour

remaining liquid into your primary fermentation vessel.

- Top up your fermentation vessel to the five gallon mark with your remaining water.
- Add in your yeast.
- Fill the small cavity on your airlock with water.
- Place your lid on your bucket.
- Gently fit your airlock into the pre-drilled hole in the bucket lid. It should be fitted with a rubber gasket to make the seal airtight. Twist the airlock into place with a gentle downward pressure to avoid damaging the seal.
- Once the lid and airlock are firmly in place, and the vessel is completely sealed, give the bucket a gentle shake to aerate the yeast and get it mixed in completely.
- Place your fermentation vessel in area that will maintain a steady temperature between 45° and 75° Fahrenheit.
- Once the initial fermentation has finished, follow the racking instructions as they are outlined above.

Spiced Mixed Berry Mead

Ingredients;

- 3lbs of honey per gallon of water, (15lbs for a 5 gallon batch) this will yield a very sweet mead, comparable to a dessert wine. You can adjust the quantity up or down depending how you like the results of the 3lbs-per-gallon recipe.
- 5 gallons of clean, room temperature water
- 1oz of dry, instant, bread yeast
- 5lbs of frozen mixed berries (Blackberries, raspberries and blueberries work best. They are frequently sold premixed under the name of mixed berry.)
- 2 vanilla beans
- 1 cinnamon stick
- 4 allspice berries

Instruction;

- Follow the instruction on whatever sanitizing product you purchased and sanitize ALL of your brewing equipment. Harmful bacteria and wild yeast strains can ruin an otherwise very successful mead.

!!!IMPORTANT!!! *If you are using aluminum pot to prepare you batch in, DO NOT USE any bleach/chlorine-based sanitizing agent. It will discolor your pot and can cause off flavors in your mead.*

- Use a sharp knife to carefully split the vanilla beans down the middle lengthwise, then, use the back of the knife to scrape the interior of the bean. Place the scrapings from the interior of the bean into your 6 gallon pot. Place the scraped beans into the linen bag, along with the remainder of the spices. Tie the bag closed and place it into the pot as well.
- Pour your still frozen berries into your 6 gallon pot
- Warm up your bottles of honey in warm tap water. You will want to make sure your containers are still tightly sealed for this step. You simply want your honey to flow easily out of the container, leaving as little behind as possible.
- Pour the warmed honey into your 6-gallon pot. *DO NOT THROW OUT THE CAP OR LID!* If you are using bottled water, use your microwave safe vessel to heat up some of your bottled water. You don't want to boil the water, simply warm it up.

Then pour it into your honey container, place whatever lid or cap it came with back on, and shake the container gently. You are trying to dissolve the last of the honey into the warm water. Then pour this water and honey into your 6-gallon pot.

- Place your 6-gallon pot on the stove and set the burner temperature to medium high. You will need to keep a close watch on your honey and water mixture, since when it starts to come to a boil, the sugars can begin to caramelize and bubble up and over the edges of your pot. This creates a huge, sticky mess, can lead to fires if you are using an open flame burner or burn you badly if it gets on your skin. Even if it doesn't cause a fire or burn you, burning your sugars can lead to strong, burnt flavors in your mead, which are undesirable.

- Once your honey and water mixture begins to boil, turn down the heat until it is just barely bubbling. Skim off any brown or discolored foam that rises to the surface. This is especially important if you are using raw or unprocessed honey, as what you see coming to the top is impurities that are harmless if consumed, but inhibit fermentation.

- Simmer your honey for between twenty minutes and one hour. Then cover the pot with a lid and let it cool to room temperature. If this mixture is poured into a plastic brew bucket while still too hot, it can damage the plastic, causing off flavors and a poorly sealing lid.

- Once your mixture has cooled to room temperature, remove the cloth bag and pour remaining liquid into your primary fermentation vessel.
- Top up your fermentation vessel to the five gallon mark with your remaining water.
- Add in your yeast.
- Fill the small cavity on your airlock with water.
- Place your lid on your bucket.
- Gently fit your airlock into the pre-drilled hole in the bucket lid. It should be fitted with a rubber gasket to make the seal airtight. Twist the airlock into place with a gentle downward pressure to avoid damaging the seal.
- Once the lid and airlock are firmly in place, and the vessel is completely sealed, give the bucket a gentle shake to aerate the yeast and get it mixed in completely.
- Place your fermentation vessel in area that will maintain a steady temperature between 45° and 75° Fahrenheit.
- Once the initial fermentation has finished, follow the racking instructions as they are outlined above.

In Closing

Congratulations, you are now making mead! While these recipes are very basic and simple, they represent the foundations on which you will be able to build if you choose to do so. Also, mastering the most basic recipes will develop your skills as a brewer and position you to be better able to craft your own recipes and execute more complex recipes from around the world.

I greatly hope that you have enjoyed your first mead making experience and that it will become a fun and rewarding hobby. My father introduced me to brewing when I was six, and I have enjoyed ever since. I hope you will as well.

www.ingramcontent.com/pod-product-compliance
Lightning Source LLC
Chambersburg PA
CBHW040251240726
48664CB00001B/351